WOLVES

Joi Washington

You can see the wolf.

eyes

You can see the eyes.

ears

You can see the ears.

nose

You can see the nose.

teeth

You can see the teeth.

tongue

You can see the tongue. 7

paws

You can see the paws.

babies

You can see the babies.

water

You can see the water.

grass

You can see the grass.

rock

You can see the rock.

rabbit

You can see the rabbit.

bear

You can see the bear.

ear

eye

nose

tail

legs

paw

You can see the wolf.

Power Words

How many can you read?

You

you

can

see

the